PIZZA
TOPPINGS

Photography by Peter Barry
Recipes originated and styled by Jacqueline Bellefontaine
Edited by Susan Dixon
Designed by Helen Johnson
Typeset by Image Setting

CLB 4455
© 1995 CLB Publishing
This edition published 1995 by Parragon Book Service Ltd
Unit 13-17 Avonbridge Trading Estate, Atlantic Road
Avonmouth, Bristol BS11 9QD
All rights reserved
ISBN 0-7525-0681-1
Printed in Hong Kong

PIZZA TOPPINGS

‖ • PARRAGON • ‖

Contents

Introduction

The exact origins of the pizza have been lost in the mists of time. It was in the sixteenth century that the tomato arrived in Europe from Mexico and had then become very popular in Italy for use with pasta. But it was not until the eighteenth century that the pizza in the form that we recognise it today first saw the light of day. Tomato-based pizzas were then made in Naples and up until 1830 were sold from open-air stalls. Pizzerias were also introduced then; they had an oven lined with bricks and volcanic rock which could reach the high temperatures required to make the best pizzas.

The popularity of the Neapolitan pizza was such that northern Italy soon became equally keen, as did first, the United States thanks to the Italian community of New York, then other parts of Europe, and finally Britain. But it has only been in the last couple of decades that the pizza has really come into its own in Britain. Both the restaurant and frozen food trades reap huge profits from pizza-making; pizzas are such a significant part of the British diet that many youngsters today find it hard to believe that they have not been around forever.

Making Pizzas at Home

There still seems to be a misconception that pizza is difficult to make at home. Not at all! Although the very high temperatures reached in the stone ovens reputed to make the best pizzas cannot be achieved in a domestic oven, excellent results are still possible. Indeed, home-made pizza is often better that the ready-made pizzas found in many shops. This may be because pizza is best eaten very fresh and suffers considerably from being kept warm or being reheated.

Fortunately, pizza is not hard to make. The traditional base is a yeast dough and our recipe uses easy-blend dried yeast which is very simple to use. Dough made with this yeast does not require proving but it is a good idea to allow it to stand in a warm place for about 15 minutes so that it begins to rise slightly before adding the topping. This is often the time taken to prepare the ingredients for the topping. If you are in a hurry and do not have time to allow the yeast to work, choose our scone-based dough which can be topped immediately.

Each recipe has a suggested dough but you can interchange them to suit your tastes and time available. Unlike other bread doughs, use ordinary plain flour rather than the strong, bread-making ones. The softer flour will give a lighter texture to the pizza base. Cooked mashed potato added to the dough will also help to give a lighter texture. Simply rub into the flour before adding the liquid to either the yeast or scone dough. About 120g/4oz of cooked potato to 225g/8oz flour is about right.

To set you on the trail of happy pizza baking, this book is packed with simple recipes for both traditional pizzas, the newer style spicy pizzas from the United States and some less familiar ones, including sweet toppings for an unusual dessert.

Principal Ingredients

Many pizzas have tomato added either in the form of a sauce or simply freshly sliced. If using fresh tomatoes, choose soft ripe fruit. Plum tomatoes or the misshapen Mediterranean ones have the best flavour. Tomato sauces are simple to make and you will find recipes using both fresh and canned tomatoes. If you make a lot of pizzas, double or treble the quantity and freeze in individual portions until required.

Cheese is another popular ingredient and is used in many of the recipes. Those which have a high fat content and which melt fast are best. The traditional cheese is Mozzarella. For authenticity choose one made from buffalo milk, now often available on supermarket shelves as well as in specialist cheese shops. Other suitable cheeses include the Italian Bel Paese or Fontina or our own Cheddar and Red Leicester.

The recipes in the book are generally given for a 23cm/9-inch or 25cm/10-inch pizza and are sufficient for 1 to 2 people. You can adjust the dough and filling ingredients proportionately to make more or fewer pizzas and can roll out the dough thicker or thinner as required. Reduce the cooking time accordingly if using a thinner dough. If you choose a thicker, deeper based pizza, add the cheese about half-way through the cooking time so that it does not burn or become tough and chewy from overcooking.

Equipment

Special equipment is not necessary; a baking sheet is fine although there are special pizza and pie trays which have holes in them to allow the heat to penetrate the dough better and to help avoid a soggy base. If using a baking sheet, prick the dough all over with a fork before adding the filling ingredients; this will have the same result.

Using a pizza cutter can make serving easier.

And finally … the test of a good pizza is in the eating. So throw away your knife and fork and use your fingers to tuck into a slice of home-made pizza.

These two pizza doughs are used to make the base of most of the pizzas in this book.

BASIC YEAST DOUGH

Yeast doughs form the basis of most traditional pizzas. This recipe uses easy-blend yeast and is quicker to prepare than most yeast doughs.

MAKES ONE 25CM/10-INCH PIZZA BASE

225g/8oz plain flour
Pinch of salt
6g/¼oz sachet easy-blend dried yeast
1 tbsp olive oil
175ml/6fl oz warm water

1. Sift the flour and salt into a warm mixing bowl and stir in the yeast.

2. Make a well in the centre, add the olive oil and enough water to mix to a soft dough. (You may not need all the water.)

3. Turn out onto a floured surface and knead for a few minutes until the dough is soft but not sticky.

4. Shape into a round ball and use as required.

TIME: Preparation takes about 15 minutes.

SCONE BASE DOUGH

A quick-to-prepare dough which is particularly well suited to a lighter, less substantial pizza.

MAKES ONE 23CM/9-INCH PIZZA BASE

225g/8oz plain flour
Pinch of salt
60g/2oz margarine
About 120ml/4fl oz milk

1. Sift the flour and salt in a mixing bowl. Rub in the margarine until the mixture resembles fine breadcrumbs.

2. Mix in enough milk to form a soft dough. (You may need not need all the milk.)

3. Shape into a smooth round ball and use as required.

TIME: Preparation takes about 10 minutes.

TOMATO SAUCES

Tomato sauces are often spread onto the base of pizzas. Fresh tomato sauce has the best flavour but you can also use the quick-to-prepare Speedy Tomato Sauce in any of the recipes.

MAKES ENOUGH FOR ONE 23-25CM/9-10-INCH PIZZA

FRESH TOMATO SAUCE

1 tbsp olive oil
½ small onion, finely chopped
1 clove garlic, crushed
340g/12oz fresh tomatoes, preferably plum, skinned, seeded and roughly chopped
2 sun-dried tomato halves in olive oil, chopped (optional)
Chopped fresh herbs (optional)

1. Heat the oil in a saucepan and fry the onion for 4 minutes until beginning to soften.
2. Stir in the garlic and continue to fry for 1 minute.
3. Add the tomatoes and bring slowly to the boil. Stir in the herbs if using.
4. Reduce the heat and simmer gently for 20-25 minutes. Use as required.

TIME: Preparation takes about 15 minutes. Cooking takes approximately 25-30 minutes.

COOK'S TIP: If you cannot find sun-dried tomatoes in olive oil, use packet sun-dried tomatoes, and soak as directed.

SPEEDY TOMATO SAUCE

1 tbsp olive oil
1 small onion, finely chopped
1 clove garlic, crushed
230g/8oz can chopped tomatoes
½ tsp dried mixed herbs

3. Add the tomatoes and herbs and bring to the boil.
4. Reduce the heat and simmer gently for 10-15 minutes. Use as required.

1. Heat the oil in a saucepan and fry the onion for 4 minutes until beginning to soften.

2. Stir in the garlic and continue to fry for 1 minute.

TIME: Preparation takes about 4 minutes and cooking takes approximately 15-20 minutes.

COOK'S TIP: Make up double or treble quantities and freeze in single portions.

11

PIZZA RUSTICA

*This classic dish from the Campanian region of Italy is almost a cross between
a pizza and a flan.*

MAKES ONE 23CM/9-INCH PIZZA

Full quantity Scone Base Dough
2 tbsps freshly grated Parmesan cheese
3 slices Parma ham
2 tomatoes, skinned, seeded and roughly
   chopped
1 hard-boiled egg, chopped
2 eggs, lightly beaten
60g/2oz Bel Paese cheese
60g/2oz Fontina or Gruyère cheese, grated
5 tbsps double cream
1 tbsp chopped fresh parsley
1 tbsp chopped fresh basil
Pinch of freshly grated nutmeg
Salt and freshly ground black pepper

1. Prepare the pizza dough according to the
recipe and roll out to form a circle about
25cm/10-inches in diameter.

2. Place the dough in a lightly oiled 23cm/9-
inch round baking dish. Fold over the edges
to form a raised border.

3. Sprinkle the base with Parmesan cheese
and place a layer of ham on top.

4. Cover the ham with a layer of chopped
tomato and egg.

5. Mix together the remaining ingredients
and pour over the pizza.

6. Bake in a preheated oven at 190°C/375°F/
Gas mark 5 for 35 minutes until golden.
Serve hot.

TIME: Preparation takes about 20 minutes. Cooking takes approximately 35 minutes.

LIGURIAN-STYLE PIZZA

The topping of this classic pizza is very similar to the Provençal dish Pissaladière.

MAKES ONE 25CM/10-INCH PIZZA

Full quantity Basic Yeast Dough
3 tbsps olive oil
340g/12oz onions, thinly sliced
2 cloves garlic, crushed
340g/12oz tomatoes, skinned, seeded and
   roughly chopped
1 tbsp tomato purée
1 tsp dried mixed herbs
Salt and freshly ground black pepper
60g/2oz can anchovy fillets, drained and cut
   in half lengthways
About 9 pitted black olives, halved

1. Prepare the pizza dough according to the recipe and roll out to form a circle a little larger than 25cm/10-inches in diameter.

2. Place the dough on a lightly oiled baking sheet. Fold over the edges to form a raised border. Allow to stand in a warm place while preparing the topping.

3. Meanwhile heat the oil in a large frying pan and fry the onion for 4-5 minutes until softened.

4. Add the garlic and continue to cook until the onion begins to brown.

5. Add the tomatoes, tomato purée and herbs. Bring gently to the boil, then reduce the heat and simmer for 15 minutes.

6. Season to taste and spoon onto the pizza base.

7. Arrange the anchovies on top of the pizza to form a criss-cross pattern.

8. Place an olive in the centre of each diamond.

9. Bake in a preheated oven at 200°C/400°F/Gas Mark 6 for 25-30 minutes or until the base is cooked and golden.

TIME: Preparation takes about 30 minutes. Cooking takes approximately 1 hour.

PIZZA QUATTRO STAGIONI (FOUR SEASONS PIZZA)

A classic pizza with no less than four different toppings.

MAKES ONE 25CM/10-INCH PIZZA

Full quantity Basic Yeast Dough
60ml/4tbsps passata (see recipe)
1st quarter
Olive oil
60g/2oz mushrooms, sliced
2nd quarter
1 slice Parma ham, cut into strips
2 pitted black olives, chopped
30g/1oz Mozzarella cheese, grated
3rd quarter
4 canned artichoke hearts, sliced
1 clove garlic, chopped
½ tsp chopped fresh oregano
Olive oil
4th quarter
30g/1oz smoked Mozzarella cheese, grated
90g/3oz mixed shellfish
5ml/1 tsp chopped fresh parsley
Olive oil
Salt and freshly ground black pepper

1. Prepare the pizza dough according to the recipe and roll out to form a circle about 25cm/10-inches in diameter.

2. Place the dough on a lightly oiled baking sheet and prick over with a fork.

3. Spread with the passata and gently mark into quarters. Allow to stand in a warm place while preparing the topping.

4. Meanwhile heat 2 tbsps olive oil in a small pan and sauté the mushrooms for 4 minutes or until just softened. Arrange on one section of the pizza.

5. Mix the Parma ham with the olives. Pile onto another section of the pizza. Sprinkle the cheese on top.

6. Arrange the artichokes on the third section of the pizza. Mix together the garlic and oregano and scatter on top. Drizzle with a little olive oil.

7. Scatter the smoked cheese on the final section of the pizza and arrange the shellfish on top. Sprinkle with parsley and drizzle with a little olive oil.

8. Season the whole pizza with salt and pepper.

9. Bake in a preheated oven at 220°C/425°F/Gas Mark 7 for 15 minutes, then reduce the heat to 190°C/375°F/Gas Mark 5 and bake for a further 20 minutes until the base is cooked and golden. Serve immediately.

TIME: Preparation takes about 30 minutes. Cooking takes approximately 40 minutes.

VARIATION: You can be particularly selective in making up your own toppings for each of the four sections.

PIZZA AI FUNGI
(PIZZA WITH MUSHROOMS)

Fresh tomato sauce, oregano and mushrooms make this a light and summery pizza.

MAKES ONE 23CM/9-INCH PIZZA

Full quantity Scone Base Dough
2 tbsps olive oil
120g/4oz mushrooms
Chopped fresh oregano
Salt and freshly ground black pepper
1 clove garlic, cut in half
Full quantity Fresh Tomato Sauce
90g/3oz Mozzarella cheese, grated
2 tbsps freshly grated Parmesan cheese

1. Prepare the pizza dough according to the recipe and roll out to form a circle about 23cm/9-inches in diameter.

2. Place the dough on a lightly oiled baking sheet and prick all over with a fork.

3. Bake in a preheated oven at 200°C/400°F/Gas Mark 6 for 15 minutes or until golden. Reduce the heat to 180°C/350°F/Gas Mark 4.

4. Heat the oil in a small pan and fry the mushrooms until soft. Stir in the oregano and season with salt and pepper.

5. Rub the pizza base with the cut edge of the garlic. Spread with the tomato sauce.

6. Arrange the mushrooms on top. Sprinkle the Mozzarella, followed by the Parmesan cheese, over the mushrooms.

7. Return to the oven and bake for 10-15 minutes or until the cheese melts.

TIME: Preparation takes about 15 minutes. Cooking takes approximately 45 minutes.

Pizza Con Cozze (Pizza with Mussels)

Seafood is in plentiful supply in Italy, and this delicious pizza is topped with mussels.

MAKES ONE 25CM/10-INCH PIZZA

680g/1½lbs mussels
Full quantity Basic Yeast Dough
280ml/10 fl oz stock or water
1 onion, cut into wedges
1 clove garlic, crushed
1 carrot, cut into chunks
1 bouquet garni
Few fresh basil leaves
Full quantity Tomato Sauce
90g/3oz Mozzarella cheese, sliced
Salt and freshly ground black pepper
Olive oil

1. Prepare the mussels. Scrub well and remove the beards. Discard any that have cracked shells or which do not close when tapped. Place the mussels in a large bowl of cold water and leave for at least 1 hour

2. Prepare the pizza dough according to the recipe and roll out to form a circle about 25cm/10-inches in diameter.

3. Place on a lightly oiled baking sheet and prick all over with a fork. Allow to stand in a warm place while preparing the topping.

4. Meanwhile put the stock, onion, garlic, carrot and bouquet garni in a large saucepan and bring to the boil. Add the mussels, cover and cook for 5 minutes or until the mussels have opened. Shake the pan or stir frequently during the cooking.

5. Remove the mussels with a draining spoon and discard any that have not opened.

6. Remove most of the mussels from the shells, reserving a few in the shells for the garnish.

7. Tear or shred the basil leaves and stir into the tomato sauce along with the mussels.

8. Spread the tomato mixture over the pizza and arrange the cheese on top. Season with salt and pepper, and drizzle with olive oil.

9. Bake in a preheated oven at 200°C/400°F/Gas Mark 6 for 25 minutes.

10. Arrange the mussels in the shells on top of the pizza and return to the oven for 5-10 minutes to heat through. Serve immediately.

TIME: Preparation takes about 30 minutes. Cooking takes approximately 40 minutes.

PIZZA NAPOLETANA

This is the classic pizza and originates from Naples.

MAKES ONE 25CM/10-INCH PIZZA

Full quantity Basic Yeast Dough
6 tomatoes, skinned and sliced
Salt and freshly ground black pepper
60g/2oz can anchovy fillets, drained
Few fresh basil leaves
90g/3oz Mozzarella cheese, sliced
Olive oil

1. Prepare the pizza dough according to the recipe and roll out to form a circle about 25cm/10-inches in diameter.

2. Place the dough on a lightly oiled baking sheet and prick all over with a fork. Allow to stand in a warm place for 15 minutes.

3. Arrange the tomato slices on top of the pizza base.

4. Season the tomatoes with a little salt and plenty of pepper.

5. Arrange the anchovies on top of the tomatoes, tear the basil leaves into pieces and scatter on top of the pizza.

6. Place the cheese on top and drizzle with a little olive oil.

7. Bake in a preheated oven at 200°C/ 400°F/Gas Mark 6 for 25-30 minutes or until the base is cooked and golden and the cheese has melted.

TIME: Preparation takes about 15 minutes. Cooking takes approximately 30 minutes.

POTATO AND ONION PIZZA

A traditional style pizza which is ideal for parties or picnics.

MAKES ONE 25CM/10-INCH PIZZA

Full quantity Basic Yeast Dough
Olive oil
340g/12oz small potatoes, peeled
2 onions, thinly sliced
Salt and freshly ground black pepper
3 cloves garlic, sliced
Small sprigs of fresh rosemary or
    1 tbsp dried rosemary

1. Prepare the pizza dough according to the recipe and roll out to form a rectangle about 28 x 18cm/11x7 inches.

2. Place the dough on a lightly oiled baking sheet and prick all over with a fork.

3. Brush the base liberally with olive oil and allow to stand in a warm place while preparing the topping.

4. Meanwhile, cook the potatoes in boiling water for 5 minutes, drain and slice thinly.

5. Arrange the onions over the base of the pizza and season well.

6. Arrange the potato slices over the onion and scatter with the garlic. Dot with sprigs of fresh rosemary or dried rosemary.

7. Drizzle olive oil all over the pizza then bake in a preheated oven at 220°C/425°F/Gas Mark 7 for 15 minutes.

8. Reduce the heat to 190°C/375°F/Gas Mark 5 and continue to cook for 25 minutes or until golden all over.

9. If the potatoes have not browned sufficiently place under a preheated grill for a few minutes.

TIME: Preparation takes about 20 minutes. Cooking takes approximately 40 minutes.

VARIATION: Spread the base with tomato sauce if liked and arrange the potatoes on top.

CALZONE
(FOLDED PIZZA)

This is a speciality from Naples and is ideal for picnics and packed lunches as it is easily transportable. You could, of course, make this as a conventional pizza, if you prefer.

MAKES 4 CALZONE

Full quantity Basic Yeast Dough
4 slices Parma Ham, cut into strips
120g/4oz Bel Paese cheese, cut into small
   pieces
2 tomatoes, sliced (optional)
Salt and freshly ground black pepper

---

1. Prepare the pizza dough according to the recipe and allow to stand in a warm place for 30 minutes or until doubled in size.

2. Knock back the dough and divide into four. Roll out each piece to form a circle about 18cm/7-inches in diameter.

3. Place a quarter of the ham, cheese and tomato on one side of each round of dough. Season with salt and pepper.

4. Dampen the edges and fold the dough over to enclose the filling. Press the edges down well to seal.

5. Place on a lightly oiled baking sheet and bake in a preheated oven at 200°C/400°F/Gas Mark 6 for about 20 minutes or until the dough is crisp and golden. Serve hot or cold.

TIME: Preparation takes about 25 minutes. Cooking takes approximately 20 minutes.

VARIATION: Add sautéed mushrooms, onions or peppers to the filling.

PIZZA AL TEGAME (FRIED PIZZA)

This method of cooking is popular in many Italian households.

MAKES ONE 20CM/8-INCH PIZZA

175g/6oz plain flour
½ tsp baking powder
Pinch of salt
30g/1oz butter
90ml/6 tbsps milk
Olive oil, for shallow frying
3 tomatoes, skinned and chopped
1 tsp capers
1 tsp chopped fresh oregano or
½ tsp dried oregano
60g/2oz Mozzarella cheese, grated

1. Sift the flour, baking powder and salt into a mixing bowl. Rub in the butter until the mixture resembles fine breadcrumbs.

2. Mix in enough milk to form a soft dough.

3. Roll out the dough to form a 20cm/8-inch round.

4. Heat enough oil to coat the bottom of a heavy-based frying pan, then cover the base with the dough. Cook over a low heat for about 5 minutes or until the underside is golden.

5. Carefully turn the pizza base over. Scatter the chopped tomatoes, capers and oregano on top of the pizza and cook for 3 minutes.

6. Sprinkle with the cheese, cover with a lid or plate and continue to cook for about 3 minutes or until the cheese melts.

TIME: Preparation takes about 10 minutes. Cooking takes approximately 10 minutes.

VARIATION: Break an egg on top of the tomatoes before covering with the cheese.

AMERICAN-STYLE SPICY BEEF PIZZA

Omit the chilli to make this a perfect pizza for kids.

MAKES ONE 25CM/10-INCH PIZZA

Full quantity Basic Yeast Dough
6oz lean minced beef
½ small onion, grated or very finely chopped
1 clove garlic, crushed
1 tsp ground allspice
1 tsp ground chilli
Sunflower oil, for frying
½ red pepper, seeded and chopped
½ green pepper, seeded and chopped
Full quantity Tomato Sauce
90g/3oz Cheddar cheese, grated

1. Prepare the pizza dough according to the recipe and roll out to form a circle about 25cm/10-inches in diameter.

2. Place the dough on a lightly oiled baking sheet, and prick all over with a fork. Allow to stand in a warm place while preparing the topping.

3. Meanwhile, put the beef, onion, garlic, allspice and chilli in a mixing bowl and mix together with your hands until well combined.

4. Shape the mixture into 18 balls, pressing it together well as you do so.

5. Shallow fry in sunflower oil for about 5 minutes until browned on all sides.

6. Place the meat balls on top of the pizza base and scatter with the chopped pepper.

7. Carefully spoon the tomato sauce over the pizza.

8. Sprinkle with the grated cheese and bake in a preheated oven at 200°C/400°F/Gas Mark 6 for 25-30 minutes or until the base is cooked and golden.

TIME: Preparation takes about 20 minutes. Cooking takes approximately 35 minutes.

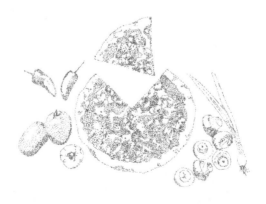

SPICY LAMB PIZZA

If you marinate the meat overnight, you can have a pizza that is very quick to prepare on the day of eating.

MAKES ONE 23CM/9-INCH PIZZA

3 tbsps dark soy sauce
1 tsp Worcestershire sauce
2 tsps sherry vinegar
1 clove garlic, crushed
½ small onion, grated or very finely chopped
¼ tsp ground cumin
¼ tsp ground coriander
1cm/½-inch piece root ginger, peeled and grated
180g/6oz lean lamb, sliced into strips
Full quantity Scone Based Dough
Full quantity Tomato Sauce
60g/2oz Cheddar cheese, grated
3 tbsps freshly grated Parmesan cheese

1. Put the soy and Worcestershire sauce, the vinegar, garlic, onion, cumin, coriander and ginger in a shallow dish and stir until well combined.

2. Add the meat, toss until well coated and marinate for at least 2 hours or overnight.

3. Prepare the pizza dough according to the recipe and roll out to form a circle about 23cm/9-inches in diameter.

4. Place the dough on a lightly oiled baking sheet and prick all over with a fork.

5. Spread the tomato sauce over the pizza base.

6. Remove the meat from the marinade with a slotted spoon and scatter over the pizza.

7. Mix together the two cheeses and sprinkle over the top of the pizza.

8. Bake in a preheated oven at 190°C/375°F/Gas Mark 5 for 35-40 minutes or until the base is cooked and the cheese has melted.

TIME: Preparation takes about 10 minutes plus marinating.
Cooking takes approximately 40 minutes.

AMERICAN HOT PIZZA
(PEPPERONI AND GREEN CHILLI PIZZA)

Hot and spicy!

MAKES ONE 25CM/10-INCHES PIZZA

Full quantity Basic Yeast Dough
60g/2oz butter
120g/4oz mushrooms, sliced
Full quantity Tomato Sauce
2 green chillies, seeded if liked, sliced into
    rings
60g/2oz pepperoni, sliced
120g/4oz Mozzarella cheese, sliced

1. Prepare the pizza dough according to the recipe and roll out to form a circle about 25cm/10-inches in diameter.

2. Place the dough on a lightly oiled baking sheet and prick all over with a fork. Allow to stand in a warm place while preparing the topping.

3. Meanwhile, melt the butter in a small saucepan and sauté the mushrooms for 2-3 minutes or until softened.

4. Spread the tomato sauce over the pizza base, then cover with the sautéed mushrooms.

5. Scatter half the chillies over the mushrooms, then top with a layer of pepperoni.

6. Lay the cheese on top and scatter with the remaining chillies.

7. Bake in a preheated oven at 200°C/400°F/ Gas Mark 6 for 25-30 minutes or until the base is cooked and golden and the cheese has melted.

TIME: Preparation takes about 25 minutes. Cooking takes approximately 35 minutes.

WATCHPOINT: If you do not like foods that are very hot, remove the seeds from the chillies as this is where most of the 'heat' is.

MEXICAN CHILLI CHICKEN

Not for the faint hearted, this is an even spicier pizza than the American Hot.

MAKES ONE 23CM/9-INCH PIZZA

Full quantity Scone Based Dough
Full quantity Tomato Sauce
2 tbsps light muscovado sugar
4 tbsps tomato ketchup
5 tbsps cider vinegar
Dash of Tabasco sauce
½-1 tsp chilli powder
1 chicken breast, skinned, boned and cut
   into small cubes
1 red chilli, seeded if liked, sliced into rings
1 green chilli, seeded if liked, sliced into
   rings
2 tbsps freshly grated Parmesan cheese

1. Prepare the pizza dough according to the recipe and roll out to form a circle about 23cm/9-inches in diameter.

2. Place the dough on a lightly oiled baking sheet and prick all over with a fork.

3. Spread the tomato sauce over the pizza base.

4. Put the sugar, ketchup, vinegar, Tabasco and chilli powder in a small saucepan and heat gently, stirring constantly until the sugar dissolves.

5. Bring to the boil and boil gently until reduced by about one third.

6. Remove from the heat and stir in the chicken. Toss until well coated in the sauce. Spoon the chicken mixture over the pizza.

7. Scatter the chillies over the top of the chicken. Sprinkle with Parmesan cheese.

8. Bake in a preheated oven at 190°C/375°F/ Gas Mark 5 for 35-40 minutes or until the base is cooked.

TIME: Preparation takes about 15 minutes. Cooking takes approximately 50 minutes.

PIZZA WITH CHILLI CON CARNE TOPPING

This is a popular pizza in the United States; it certainly makes a tasty and filling meal.

MAKES ONE 25CM/10-INCH PIZZA

Full quantity Basic Yeast Dough
1 tbsp sunflower oil
½ small onion
1 clove garlic, crushed
1 green chilli, chopped
150g/5oz lean minced beef
Pinch of chilli powder
200g/7oz can red kidney beans, drained and
    rinsed
230g/8oz can chopped tomatoes
60g/2oz smoked Cheddar cheese, grated

1. Prepare the pizza dough according to the recipe and roll out to form a circle about 25cm/10-inches in diameter.

2. Place on an oiled baking sheet and prick all over with a fork. Allow to stand in a warm place while preparing the topping.

3. Meanwhile, heat the oil in a saucepan and fry the onion, garlic and green chilli until soft.

4. Add the minced beef and continue to cook until browned.

5. Stir in the chilli powder and cook for 1 minute.

6. Add the beans to the pan along with the tomatoes.

7. Bring gently to the boil, then reduce the heat and simmer gently for 15 minutes.

8. Spread over the pizza base and sprinkle with the grated cheese.

9. Bake in a preheated oven at 200°C/400°F/Gas Mark 6 for 25-30 minutes or until the base is cooked and golden and the cheese has melted.

TIME: Preparation takes about 25 minutes. Cooking takes approximately 50 minutes.

VARIATION: Use a mature Cheddar or other strong flavoured cheese if liked.

PIZZA CHICKEN TIKKA

As people become increasingly familiar with different cuisines, so everyone can have fun experimenting and mixing styles, as in this unusual main-meal pizza.

MAKES ONE 25CM/10-INCH PIZZA

140ml/¼ pint natural yogurt
2.5cm/1-inch piece root ginger, peeled and
    grated
1 clove garlic, crushed
1 tsp chilli powder
½ tsp ground turmeric
2 tsps ground coriander
Salt and freshly ground black pepper
4 tsps lemon juice
2 tbsps sunflower oil
2 chicken breasts, skinned and boned
Full quantity of Basic Yeast Dough
Full quantity Tomato Sauce
½ green pepper, seeded and chopped
Fresh coriander sprigs and lemon wedges,
    to garnish

---

1. Mix together the yogurt, ginger, garlic, chilli, turmeric, coriander, salt, pepper, lemon juice and oil in a shallow dish.

2. Add the chicken and toss until well coated. Cover and leave to marinate in a refrigerator for at least 6 hours, or overnight.

3. Prepare the pizza dough according to the recipe and roll out to form a circle a little larger than 25cm/10-inches in diameter.

4. Place the dough on a lightly oiled baking sheet. Fold over the edges to form a raised border. Allow to stand in a warm place for 15 minutes.

5. Spread the tomato sauce over the base and bake in a preheated oven at 200°C/400°F/Gas Mark 6 for 10 minutes.

6. Remove from the oven, spoon over the chicken and the marinade, and scatter the chopped pepper over the top.

7. Return to the oven and bake for 15-20 minutes or until base is golden and the chicken is cooked.

8. Serve garnished with sprigs of coriander and lemon wedges.

TIME: Preparation takes about 15 minutes plus marinating. Cooking takes approximately 35 minutes.

41

CHICKEN PIZZA WITH THAI SPICES

Spicy chicken and sweet yellow peppers top this Oriental-style pizza.

MAKES ONE 23CM/9-INCH PIZZA

Full quantity Scone Based Dough
1 Chicken breast, skinned, boned and cut
　　into strips
2 tbsps sunflower oil
½ yellow pepper, seeded and chopped
30g/1oz butter
60g/2oz button mushrooms
2 tsps Thai 7-spice
Bunch of spring onions, cut into 2.5cm/
　　1-inch lengths
Full quantity Tomato Sauce
3 processed cheese slices, cut into strips
Sprigs fresh coriander, to garnish

1. Prepare pizza dough according to the recipe and roll out to form a circle about 23cm/9-inches in diameter.

2. Place the dough on a lightly oiled baking sheet and prick all over with a fork.

3. Bake in a preheated oven at 200°C/400°F/ Gas Mark 6 for 15 minutes or until golden-brown. Reduce the heat to 180°C/350°F/Gas Mark 4.

4. Meanwhile, heat the oil in a frying pan and fry the pepper for 5 minutes until just beginning to soften. Remove with a draining spoon and set aside.

5. Add the butter and stir until melted, sauté the mushrooms for 2 minutes, remove and set aside.

6. Add the Thai 7-spice and cook over a low heat for 1 minute.

7. Stir in the chicken and toss until well coated, then increase the heat and cook until the chicken begins to brown.

8. Return the mushrooms to the pan, add the spring onions, toss together, then remove from the heat.

9. Spread the tomato sauce over the part-cooked pizza base. Sprinkle with half the chopped pepper. Spread the chicken mixture over the pizza.

10. Sprinkle with the remaining chopped pepper and the cheese.

11. Return to the oven and bake for 10-15 minutes until the base is cooked and golden.

12. Serve garnished with fresh coriander.

TIME: Preparation takes about 20 minutes. Cooking takes approximately 45 minutes.

SPICY VEGETARIAN PIZZA

A wholesome vegetarian pizza, very rich in flavour.

MAKES ONE 25CM/10-INCH PIZZA

Full quantity Basic Yeast Dough
60ml/4 tbsps olive oil
1 large onion, chopped
2 cloves garlic, crushed
1 red chilli, seeded and chopped
1 green chilli, seeded and chopped
400g/14oz can chopped tomatoes
Dash of Tabasco (optional)
½ red pepper, seeded
½ green pepper, seeded
½ yellow pepper, seeded
90g/3oz mushrooms, sliced
Chopped fresh marjoram or ½ tsp dried
    marjoram
60g/2oz Cheddar cheese, grated
60g/2oz Red Leicester cheese, grated

1. Prepare the pizza dough according to the recipe and roll out to form a circle about 25cm/10-inches in diameter.

2. Place the dough on a lightly oiled baking sheet and prick all over with a fork. Allow to stand in a warm place while preparing the topping.

3. Meanwhile, heat 2 tbsps of the oil in a saucepan and fry the onion, garlic and chillies for about 5 minutes or until softened.

4. Stir in the tomatoes, Tabasco if using, and bring to the boil, then reduce the heat and simmer gently for 15 minutes.

5. Meanwhile, slice 1 or 2 rings from the peppers and set aside. Chop the remaining peppers.

6. Heat the remaining oil in a frying pan and fry the chopped peppers for 2 minutes. Add the mushrooms and continue to cook for 3 minutes.

7. Spread the tomato sauce over the pizza base and cover with the sautéed peppers and mushrooms.

8. Mix together the marjoram and cheeses and sprinkle over the pizza.

9. Top with the reserved pepper rings and brush the rings with a little extra oil.

10. Bake in a preheated oven at 200°C/400°F/Gas Mark 6 for 25-30 minutes or until the base is cooked and golden.

TIME: Preparation takes about 20 minutes. Cooking takes approximately 1 hour.

VARIATION: Vary the degree of hotness of this pizza by adding more or less chillies.

PIZZA WITH SPICY SAUSAGE MEAT

An unusual way of combining both East and West.

MAKES ONE 23CM/9-INCH PIZZA

Full quantity Scone Based Pizza Dough
Full quantity Tomato Sauce
1 tbsp olive oil
225g/8oz sausage meat
1-2 tsps Chinese five-spice powder
Salt and freshly ground black pepper
60g/2oz canned pimentos, roughly chopped
60g/2oz Edam cheese, grated

1. Prepare the pizza dough according to the recipe and roll out to form a circle about 23cm/9-inches in diameter.

2. Place the dough on a lightly oiled baking sheet and prick all over with a fork.

3. Spread the tomato sauce over the pizza base.

4. Heat the oil in a frying pan and fry the sausage-meat for 5 minutes, until browned. Break up the sausage meat as it cooks with the side of a wooden spoon.

5. Stir in the spices and continue to cook for 2 minutes. Season with salt and pepper. Stir in the pimentos

6. Spread the sausage-meat mixture over the pizza. Sprinkle with the grated cheese

7. Bake in a preheated oven at 190°C/375°F/ Gas Mark 5 for 35-40 minutes or until the base is cooked.

TIME: Preparation takes about 5 minutes. Cooking takes approximately 55 minutes.

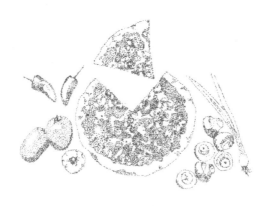

MEAT FEAST

Arrange the meat in sections on the pizza or simply scatter over randomly.

MAKES ONE 25CM/10-INCH PIZZA

Full quantity Basic Yeast Dough
Full quantity Tomato Sauce
60g/2oz mushrooms, sliced
120g/4oz selection of sliced meats, e.g.
   salami, pepperoni, garlic sausage, ham or
   pastrami
60g/2oz Mozzarella cheese, grated
Olive oil
Salt and freshly ground black pepper

1. Prepare the pizza dough according to the recipe and roll out to form a circle about 25cm/10-inches in diameter.

2. Place the dough on a lightly oiled baking sheet and prick all over with a fork. Allow to stand in a warm place for 15 minutes.

3. Spread the tomato sauce over the pizza base and scatter the mushrooms on top.

4. Cut large slices of meat into smaller pieces and arrange the meats on the pizza. Sprinkle with the grated cheese.

5. Drizzle with olive oil and season with salt and pepper.

6. Bake in a preheated oven at 200°C/400°F/Gas Mark 6 for 15 minutes, then reduce the heat to 190°C/375°F/Gas Mark 5 and bake for a further 20 minutes or until the base is cooked and golden.

TIME: Preparation takes about 10 minutes. Cooking takes approximately 30 minutes.

WATCHPOINT: If the meat begins to dry out, cover the pizza with a loose tent of foil.

ONION AND SALAMI PIZZA

You can use any type of salami on this pizza. Milano is a good choice or try a peppered salami for extra zip.

MAKES ONE 25CM/10-INCH PIZZA

Full quantity Basic Yeast Dough
Full quantity Tomato Sauce
3 tbsps olive oil
460g/1lb onions, sliced
1 tsp sugar
60g/2oz salami, sliced
30g/1oz pimento-stuffed olives
Chopped fresh marjoram

1. Prepare the pizza dough according to the recipe and roll out to form a circle about 25cm/10-inches in diameter.

2. Place the dough on a lightly oiled baking sheet and prick all over with a fork.

3. Spread the tomato sauce over the pizza base and leave to stand in a warm place while preparing the rest of the topping.

4. Meanwhile, heat the oil in a large frying pan and fry the onions until beginning to soften.

5. Sprinkle the sugar onto the onions and continue to cook over a low heat for about 15 minutes until the onions begin to caramelize and turn golden brown.

6. Spread the onions on top of the tomato and top with the salami and olives.

7. Sprinkle with a little chopped marjoram.

8. Bake in a preheated oven at 200°C/400°F/ Gas Mark 6 for 25-30 minutes or until the base is cooked and golden.

TIME: Preparation takes about 15 minutes. Cooking takes approximately 50 minutes.

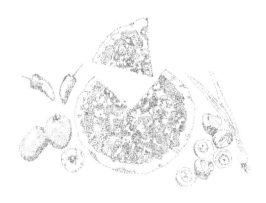

BOLOGNESE TOPPED PIZZA

A popular choice with teenagers.

MAKES ONE 23CM/9-INCH PIZZA

Full quantity Scone Based Dough
1 tbsp olive oil
1 small onion, sliced
225g/8oz lean minced beef
1 clove garlic, crushed
60g/2oz mushrooms, sliced
230g/8oz can chopped tomatoes
½ tsp dried mixed herbs
1 tbsp tomato purée
Salt and freshly ground black pepper
3 tbsps Mascarpone cheese
4 tbsps freshly grated Parmesan cheese

---

1. Prepare the pizza dough according to the recipe and roll out to form a circle about 23cm/9-inches in diameter.

2. Place the dough on a lightly oiled baking sheet and prick all over with a fork.

3. Bake in a preheated oven at 200°C/400°F/ Gas Mark 6 for 15 minutes or until golden. Reduce the heat to 180°C/350°F/Gas Mark 4.

4. Meanwhile, heat the oil in a large frying pan and fry the onion for 3-4 minutes until beginning to brown.

5. Add the minced beef and garlic and toss well. Cook over a high heat for 5 minutes until browned.

6. Reduce the heat and stir in the mushrooms, tomatoes, herbs, tomato purée and seasoning. Cover and simmer gently for 10 minutes.

7. Spread the Mascarpone cheese over the base of the pizza and spoon the Bolognese sauce on top, leaving a border of the cheese around the edge.

8. Return to the oven and bake for 10-15 minutes until the cheese has melted..

9. Sprinkle with Parmesan cheese and serve immediately.

TIME: Preparation takes about 20 minutes. Cooking takes approximately 50 minutes.

SPINACH AND HAM PIZZA

A colourful and unusual pizza topping which is ideal for parties.

MAKES ONE 23CM/9-INCH PIZZA

Full quantity Scone Based Dough
2 tbsps sunflower oil
1 onion, chopped
1 clove garlic, crushed
225g/8oz chopped spinach, frozen
Salt and freshly ground black pepper
Pinch of freshly grated nutmeg
Full quantity Tomato Sauce
2 tbsps pine nuts
60g/2oz Parma ham
90g/3oz Mozzarella cheese, sliced
Olive oil

1. Prepare the pizza dough according to the recipe and roll out to form a circle about 23cm/9-inches in diameter.

2. Place the dough on a lightly oiled baking sheet and prick all over with a fork.

3. Bake in a preheated oven at 200°C/400°F/Gas Mark 6 for 15 minutes or until golden. Reduce the heat to 180°C/350°F/Gas Mark 4.

4. Meanwhile, heat the oil in a saucepan and fry the onion for 4 minutes until beginning to soften.

5. Add the garlic and fry for 1 minute.

6. Reduce the heat and add the frozen spinach. Cook over a very low heat until it has thawed, stirring occasionally. Increase the heat and boil off any liquid. Season with salt, pepper and nutmeg.

7. Spread the tomato sauce over the part cooked pizza base, then spoon over the spinach mixture. Scatter half the pine nuts on top of the spinach.

8. Crinkle up the Parma ham and arrange on top of the pizza along with the cheese.

9. Brush the ham with a little extra oil and top with the remaining pine nuts.

10. Return to the oven and bake for 10-15 minutes until the cheese has melted.

TIME: Preparation takes about 20 minutes. Cooking takes approximately 40 minutes.

PIZZA WITH GARLIC SAUSAGE

A colourful and very moreish pizza.

MAKES ONE 25CM/10-INCH PIZZA

Full quantity Basic Yeast Dough
Full quantity Tomato Sauce
30ml/2 tbsps olive oil
½ red pepper, seeded and cut into rings
½ green pepper, seeded and cut into rings
½ yellow pepper, seeded and cut into rings
120g/4oz garlic sausage, sliced
120g/4oz Mozzarella cheese, grated
6 pitted black olives, sliced

1. Prepare the pizza dough according to the recipe and roll out to form a circle about 25cm/10-inches in diameter.

2. Place the dough on a lightly oiled baking sheet and prick all over with a fork.

3. Spread the pizza base with the tomato sauce and allow to stand in a warm place while preparing the topping.

4. Meanwhile, heat the oil in a large frying pan and fry the peppers for 5 minutes, stirring constantly until just softened.

5. Make a ring of garlic sausage around the outside of the pizza. Make another ring of peppers, alternating the colours.

6. Place remaining rings in the centre of the pizza.

7. Sprinkle with the cheese and top with the olives.

8. Bake in a preheated oven at 200°C/400°F/ Gas Mark 6 for 25-30 minutes or until the base is cooked and golden.

TIME: Preparation takes about 10 minutes. Cooking takes approximately 40 minutes.

HAM AND ASPARAGUS PIZZA WHEEL

Asparagus gives this pizza a touch of luxury and a wonderfully fresh taste.

MAKES ONE 25CM/10-INCH PIZZA

Full quantity Basic Yeast Dough
12 asparagus spears, trimmed
Full quantity Fresh Tomato Sauce
6 thin slices ham
60g/2oz Dolcelatte cheese, crumbled
60g/2oz Bel Paese cheese
60ml/4 tbsps Mascarpone cheese
2 tbsps milk
Salt and freshly ground black pepper

1. Prepare the pizza dough according to the recipe and roll out to form a circle about 25cm/10-inches in diameter.

2. Place the dough on a lightly oiled baking sheet and prick all over with a fork. Allow to stand in a warm place while preparing the topping.

3. Meanwhile, bring a frying pan of water to the boil and add the asparagus. Cook for 4 minutes, then remove from the pan and plunge into cold water to prevent any further cooking.

4. Spread the tomato sauce over the pizza base.

5. Spread the ham slices out on a work surface. Sprinkle the Dolcelatte cheese along one side of each ham slice.

6. Roll up each slice of ham to form a cigar shape and arrange on top of the pizza like the spokes of a wheel.

7. Drain the asparagus well and arrange in between the rolls of ham.

8. Beat the Bel Paese until slightly softened, then beat in the Mascarpone and milk. Pour over the top of the pizza.

9. Season with salt and pepper and bake in a preheated oven at 200°C/400°F/Gas Mark 6 for 25-30 minutes or until the base is cooked and golden.

TIME: Preparation takes about 15 minutes. Cooking takes approximately 35 minutes.

PIZZA SAUSAGE BEANO

A favourite with the kids, making use of many popular ingredients.

MAKES ONE 23CM/9-INCH PIZZA

Full quantity Scone Base Dough
2 pork and beef sausages
230g/8oz can chopped tomatoes with herbs
200g/7oz can baked beans in tomato sauce
1 tsp brown fruity sauce
30g/1oz Cheddar cheese, grated
60g/2oz Mozzarella cheese, grated
3 rashers streaky bacon, rinds removed and
   cut into thin strips

1. Prepare the pizza dough according to the recipe and roll out to form a circle a little larger than 23cm/9-inches in diameter.

2. Place the dough on a lightly oiled baking sheet. Fold over the edges to form a raised border.

3. Dry fry or grill the sausages until cooked and golden. Allow to cool slightly, then slice.

4. Mix together the tomatoes, beans and brown fruity sauce until well combined. Stir in the sausages.

5. Spoon the sausage mixture over the pizza base and sprinkle with the cheeses.

6. Arrange the strips of bacon in a criss-cross pattern over the top of the pizza.

7. Bake in a preheated oven at 200°C/400°F/ Gas Mark 6 for 20-25 minutes or until the base is cooked and golden.

TIME: Preparation takes about 10 minutes. Cooking takes approximately 30 minutes.

TROPICANA
(PIZZA WITH HAM AND PINEAPPLE)

A popular pizza which is very simple to prepare.

MAKES ONE 23CM/9-INCH PIZZA

Full quantity Scone Based Dough
Full quantity Tomato Sauce
Pinch of ground allspice
2 thick slices ham, cut into strips and then squares
60g/2oz canned pineapple chunks, drained weight
Salt and freshly ground black pepper
Chopped fresh oregano
120g/4oz Mozzarella cheese, grated

1. Prepare the pizza dough according to the recipe and roll out to form a circle about 23cm/9-inches in diameter.

2. Place the dough on a lightly oiled baking sheet and prick all over with a fork.

3. Spread the tomato sauce over the pizza dough and sprinkle with a generous pinch of allspice.

4. Arrange the ham and pineapple on top of the tomato sauce.

5. Season with salt and pepper, then sprinkle with the oregano and grated cheese.

6. Bake in a preheated oven at 190°C/375°F/ Gas Mark 5 for 35-40 minutes or until the base is cooked.

TIME: Preparation takes about 5 minutes. Cooking takes approximately 40 minutes.

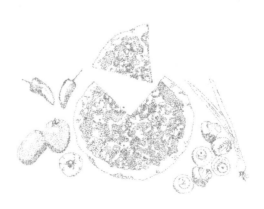

PIZZA WITH SWEET PEPPERS AND SUN-DRIED TOMATOES

This pizza has a fresh, gutsy flavour and is reminiscent of hot Mediterranean summers.

MAKES ONE 25CM/10-INCH PIZZA

1 red pepper
1 yellow pepper
1 green pepper
Olive oil
Full quantity Basic Yeast Dough
6 sun-dried tomato halves in olive oil, cut
    into halves or quarters
60g/2oz salami, cut into strips
2 cloves garlic, chopped
Few fresh basil leaves
90g/3oz ricotta cheese
Salt and freshly ground black pepper

1. Cut the peppers in half and remove the stems, cores and seeds. Flatten the peppers with the palm of your hand and brush the skins with olive oil.

2. Place the peppers, skin side up, under a pre-heated grill. Cook about 5cm/2-inches away from the heat source until the skins are well blistered and charred.

3. Wrap the peppers in a clean tea-towel and leave for 15 minutes. Peel off the charred skins with a small vegetable knife, and slice.

4. Make the pizza dough according to the recipe and roll out to form a circle about 25cm/10-inches in diameter.

5. Place the dough on a lightly oiled baking sheet and prick all over with a fork. Allow to stand in a warm place for 15 minutes.

6. Scatter the sliced peppers randomly over the pizza base. Arrange the sun-dried tomatoes on top.

7. Scatter the Salami over the pizza along with the chopped garlic.

8. Tear the basil leaves into pieces and scatter on top. Place blobs of cheese over the pizza and season well.

9. Drizzle with olive oil and bake in a preheated oven at 200°C/400°F/Gas Mark 6 for 25-30 minutes or until the base is cooked and golden.

TIME: Preparation takes about 40 minutes. Cooking takes approximately 30 minutes.

PIZZA WITH MIXED SEAFOOD

Look out for packs of mixed seafood in the chiller or frozen food cabinets of your local supermarket.

MAKES ONE 23CM/9-INCH PIZZA

Full quantity Scone Base Dough
Full quantity Tomato Sauce, preferably fresh
60g/2oz can anchovy fillets, drained
175g/6oz mixed seafood, eg prawns,
   mussels, clams, squid etc
2 tsps capers
60g/2oz Bel Paese cheese
60g/2oz full-fat cream cheese

1. Prepare pizza dough according to the recipe and roll out to form a circle about 23cm/9-inches in diameter.

2. Place the dough on a lightly oiled baking sheet and prick all over with a fork.

3. Bake in a preheated oven at 200°C/400°F/ Gas Mark 6 for 15 minutes or until golden. Reduce the heat to 180°C/350°F/Gas Mark 4.

4. Spread the tomato sauce over the pizza base and arrange the anchovies on top or scatter randomly.

5. Place the seafood on top and sprinkle with the capers.

6. Beat together the Bel Paesé and cream cheese until well combined.

7. Place blobs of the cheese mixture over the pizza, then return to the oven and bake for 10 minutes until the cheeses have melted.

TIME: Preparation takes about 10 minutes. Cooking takes approximately 25 minutes.

TUNA AND PRAWN PROVENÇAL PIZZA

Another pizza with a fresh Mediterranean feel to it.

MAKES ONE 25CM/10-INCH PIZZA

Full quantity Basic Yeast Dough
2 tbsps olive oil
½ large onion, sliced
1 clove garlic, crushed
1 courgette, sliced
200g/7oz can chopped tomatoes
1 tbsp tomato purée
½ tsp dried herbs de Provence
Salt and freshly ground black pepper
90g/3oz cooked and peeled prawns
180g/6oz can tuna, drained
90g/3oz Saint Paulin cheese, sliced

1. Prepare the pizza dough according to the recipe and roll out to form a circle a little larger than 25cm/10-inches in diameter.

2. Place the dough on a lightly oiled baking sheet. Fold over the edges to form a raised border. Allow to stand in a warm place while preparing the topping.

3. Meanwhile, heat the oil in a saucepan and fry the onion for 5 minutes until softened and beginning to brown.

4. Add the garlic and cook for a further minute. Stir in the courgette and fry for 3 minutes.

5. Stir in the tomatoes, tomato purée, herbs and seasoning. Bring to the boil, then reduce the heat and simmer gently for 10-15 minutes.

6. Spread the mixture over the pizza base.

7. Scatter the prawns over the surface of the pizza.

8. Flake the tuna into chunks and place on top of the pizza.

9. Arrange the cheese on top and bake in a preheated oven at 200°C/400°F/Gas Mark 6 for 25-30 minutes or until the base is cooked and golden.

TIME: Preparation takes about 15 minutes. Cooking takes approximately 40 minutes.

SARDINE AND TOMATO PIZZA

Arranging the sardines like the spokes of a wheel makes for a very attractive pizza which is also simple and quick to prepare.

MAKES ONE 23CM/9-INCH PIZZA

Full quantity Scone Based Dough
Full quantity Tomato Sauce
120g/4oz can sardines, drained
1 tbsp chopped fresh parsley
60g/2oz Swiss Emmental cheese, grated

1. Prepare pizza dough according to the recipe and roll out to form a circle about 23cm/9-inches in diameter.

2. Place the dough on a lightly oiled baking sheet and prick all over with a fork.

3. Bake in a preheated oven at 200°C/400°F/Gas Mark 6 for 15 minutes or until golden. Reduce the heat to 180°C/350°F/Gas Mark 4.

4. Spread the tomato sauce over the part-baked base and arrange the sardines on top.

5. Sprinkle with the parsley and then the cheese.

6. Return to the oven and bake for 10-15 minutes until the base is golden and the cheese has melted.

TIME: Preparation takes about 10 minutes. Cooking takes approximately 30 minutes.

TASTY TUNA PIZZA

A substantial pizza using ingredients from several European countries.

MAKES ONE 25CM/10-INCH PIZZA

Full quantity Basic Yeast Dough
2 beef tomatoes, sliced
1 red onion, sliced
180g/6oz can tuna, drained
1 hard boiled egg, cut into wedges
120g/4oz feta cheese, cubed
8 pitted black olives
3 tbsps olive oil
1 tbsp white wine vinegar
Salt and freshly ground black pepper
Few fresh basil leaves, to garnish

1. Prepare the pizza dough according to the recipe and roll out to form a circle about 25cm/10-inches in diameter.

2. Place the dough on a lightly oiled baking sheet and prick all over with a fork. Allow to stand in a warm place for 15 minutes.

3. Arrange the tomato slices and onion on top of the pizza base.

Bake in a preheated oven at 200°C/400°F/ Gas Mark 6 for 10 minutes.

4. Break the tuna into chunks and place on top of the pizza.

5. Arrange the egg wedges on the pizza along with the cheese and olives.

6. Whisk together the oil, vinegar, and seasoning with a fork and sprinkle over the pizza.

7. Bake for 15 to 20 minutes or until the base is cooked and golden.

8. Top with basil leaves.

TIME: Preparation takes about 30 minutes. Cooking takes approximately 30 minutes.

PIZZA WITH SPANISH STYLE SEAFOOD

*This pizza is topped with a mixture of seafood and chicken pieces
lightly flavoured with saffron.*

MAKES ONE 25CM/10-INCH PIZZA

2 tbsps white wine
Few strands saffron
Full quantity Basic Yeast Dough
Full quantity Tomato Sauce
3 tbsps olive oil
1 onion, sliced
1 clove garlic, crushed
1 chicken breast, skinned, boned and sliced
½ red pepper, seeded and sliced
1 bay leaf
120g/4oz mixed seafood
2 tbsps frozen peas
60g/2oz Mozzarella cheese, sliced

1. Put the wine in a small dish, add the saffron and allow to stand for at least 30 minutes.

2. Prepare the pizza dough according to the recipe and roll out to form a circle a little larger than 25cm/10 inches in diameter.

3. Place the dough on a lightly oiled baking sheet. Fold over the edges to form a raised border. Allow to stand in a warm place for 15 minutes.

4. Spread the tomato sauce over the base and bake in a preheated oven at 200°C/400°F/Gas Mark 6 for 10 minutes.

5. Meanwhile, heat the oil in a frying pan and fry the onion until beginning to soften.

6. Add the garlic, chicken and red pepper and fry for 2 minutes. Add the wine, saffron and bay leaf and cook for 4 minutes, until the chicken is just cooked.

7. Stir in the seafood and frozen peas.

8. Remove the bay leaf and spoon the mixture over the pizza. Top with the cheese.

9. Bake in a preheated oven at 200°C/400°F/Gas Mark 6 for 15-20 minutes or until the base is cooked and golden.

TIME: Preparation takes about 20 minutes. Cooking takes approximately 40 minutes.

PRAWN, BACON AND AVOCADO PIZZA

This delicious blend of seafood, meat and avocado makes the best of all worlds.

MAKES ONE 25CM/10-INCH PIZZA

Full quantity Basic Yeast Dough
Full quantity Tomato Sauce
1 ripe avocado
Lemon juice
4 rashers smoked streaky bacon, rinds
    removed and chopped
120g/4oz cooked and peeled prawns
90g/3oz Mozzarella cheese, grated
4-8 whole prawns (optional)

1. Prepare the pizza dough according to the recipe and roll out to form a circle about 25cm/10-inches in diameter.

2. Place the dough on a lightly oiled baking sheet and prick all over with a fork.

3. Spread the base with the tomato sauce and allow to stand in a warm place while preparing the rest of the topping.

4. Meanwhile, cut the avocado in half and remove the stone. Peel one half and slice, toss in lemon juice and set aside. Peel and chop the other half and toss in lemon juice.

5. Bake the pizza base in a preheated oven at 200°C/400°F/Gas Mark 6 for 10 minutes, then scatter the chopped avocado, bacon and peeled prawns over the surface of the pizza.

6. Arrange the sliced avocado on top. Sprinkle with the cheese.

7. Arrange whole prawns on top if using, and bake for 15-10 minutes or until the base is cooked and golden.

TIME: Preparation takes about 15 minutes. Cooking takes approximately 30 minutes.

CLASSIC VEGETARIAN PIZZA

A thick base topped and overflowing with lots of freshly prepared vegetables.

MAKES ONE 25CM/10-INCH PIZZA

Full quantity Basic Yeast Dough
90ml/6 tbsps passata
2 tbsps olive oil
1 large onion, cut into wedges
1 clove garlic, crushed
½ red pepper, seeded and sliced
½ green pepper seeded and sliced
2 tomatoes, sliced
60g/2oz mushrooms, sliced
60ml/4 tbsps sweetcorn kernels
Chopped fresh oregano
Chopped fresh marjoram
Salt and freshly ground black pepper
60g/2oz Mozzarella cheese, sliced
60g/2oz smoked Mozzarella cheese, sliced

1. Prepare the pizza dough according to the recipe and roll out to form a circle about 25cm/10-inches in diameter.

2. Place the dough on a lightly oiled baking sheet. Fold over the edges to form a raised border.

3. Spread the passata over the base and allow to stand in a warm place while preparing the topping.

4. Meanwhile, heat the oil in a frying pan and fry the onion for 4 minutes until just softened. Add the garlic and cook for another minute.

5. Place the mixture on top of the pizza.

6. Add the peppers to the pan and sauté for 2 minutes then arrange on top of the pizza.

7. Top the pizza with the remaining vegetables and sprinkle with plenty of fresh herbs. Season well.

8. Arrange the cheeses on top of the vegetables and bake in a preheated oven at 200°C/400°F/Gas Mark 6 for 25-30 minutes or until the base is cooked and golden.

TIME: Preparation takes about 30 minutes. Cooking takes approximately 30 minutes.

VARIATION: Add a selection of any vegetables that you have in the fridge.

WILD MUSHROOM PIZZA WITH TWO CHEESES

Wild mushrooms give a lift to this simple pizza, making it rather special.

MAKES ONE 25CM/10-INCH PIZZA

Full quantity Basic Yeast Dough
60ml/4 tbsps red pesto
30g/1oz butter
2 tbsps olive oil
1 clove garlic
60g/2oz shiitake mushrooms, sliced
60g/2oz oyster mushrooms, sliced
60g/2oz yellow oyster mushrooms, sliced
60g/2oz brown cap mushrooms, sliced
60g/2oz Brie
60g/2oz goat's cheese

1. Prepare the pizza dough according to the recipe and roll out to form a circle about 25cm/10-inch in diameter.

2. Place the dough on a lightly oiled baking sheet and prick all over with a fork.

3. Spread the red pesto over the base and allow to stand in a warm place while preparing the topping.

4. Meanwhile, melt the butter with the oil and garlic clove in a large saucepan and sauté the mushrooms for 2-4 minutes, tossing frequently. Remove the garlic and discard. Scatter the mushrooms over the pizza base.

5. Remove the rind from the cheese and discard. Slice the cheese and arrange on top of the pizza.

6. Bake in a preheated oven at 200°C/400°F/Gas Mark 6 for 25-30 minutes or until the base is cooked and golden.

TIME: Preparation takes about 10 minutes. Cooking time approximately 35 minutes.

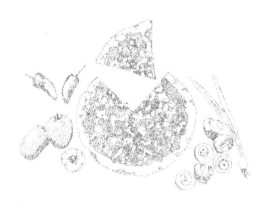

PIZZA WITH ARTICHOKES

Easy to prepare, this is an ideal pizza for party nibbles.

MAKES ONE 23CM/9-INCH PIZZA

Full quantity Scone Based Dough
60ml/4 tbsps passata
1 tbsp Worcestershire sauce
Tabasco
400g/15oz can artichoke hearts, drained and
    halved
4 plum tomatoes, skinned, seeded and
    chopped
1 clove garlic, chopped
2 tbsps chopped parsley
30g/1oz Bel Paese cheese, cut into small
    cubes
30g/1oz Fontina cheese, grated

1. Prepare the pizza dough according to the recipe and roll out to form about 23cm/9-inches in diameter.

2. Place the dough on a lightly oiled baking sheet and prick all over with a fork.

3. Bake in a preheated oven at 200°C/400°F/ Gas Mark 6 for 15 minutes or until golden. Reduce the heat to 180°C/350°F/Gas Mark 4.

4. Mix together the passata, Worcestershire sauce and a few drops of Tabasco and spread over the part-cooked base.

5. Arrange the artichoke hearts on top of the tomato mixture. Scatter the chopped tomatoes over the artichokes.

6. Sprinkle the pizza with the garlic and parsley, and top with the two cheeses.

7. Return to the oven and bake for 10-15 minutes until the cheese has melted.

TIME: Preparation takes about 15 minutes. Cooking takes approximately 30 minutes.

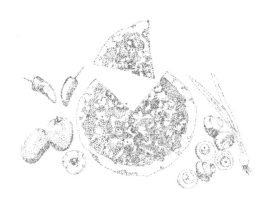

EGG TOMATO PIZZA

The potato added to the base results in a lighter texture base.
This super pizza can be served hot or cold.

MAKES ONE 23CM/9-INCH PIZZA

225g/8oz plain flour
Pinch of salt
1 tsp baking powder
½ tsp dried mixed herbs
120g/4oz cooked potatoes, mashed
30g/1oz margarine
About 60ml/4 tbsps milk
60ml/4 tbsps olive oil
60ml/4 tbsps tomato chutney
2 hard-boiled eggs, sliced
2 tomatoes, sliced
6 pimento stuffed olives, sliced
Freshly ground black pepper
90g/3oz Gruyère cheese, grated

1. Sift the flour and salt into a mixing bowl and stir in the baking powder and herbs.

2. Rub in the potatoes and margarine.

3. Mix in enough milk to form a firm dough.

4. Roll out to form a 23cm/9-inches circle.

5. Heat half the oil in a large, heavy-based frying pan and fry the pizza base for 4-5 minutes or until golden. Slide out of the pan.

6. Add the remaining oil and return the pizza base, flipping over to cook the other side.

7. Spread the tomato chutney over the base and arrange the sliced eggs and tomatoes on top.

8. Scatter with the olives and season with pepper.

9. Sprinkle with the cheese and place under a preheated medium grill for 4-5 minutes or until the cheese melts.

TIME: Preparation takes about 20 minutes. Cooking takes approximately 15 minutes.

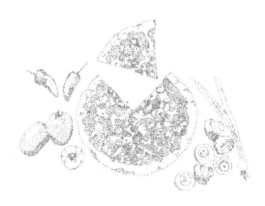

ROAST AUBERGINE AND TOMATO PIZZA

This mouth-watering pizza is perfect for cold nights by the fire.

MAKES ONE 25CM/10-INCH PIZZA

---

1 large aubergine
Salt
Full quantity Basic Yeast Dough
90ml/6 tbsps passata
Olive oil
2 beef tomatoes, sliced
2 cloves garlic, sliced
Freshly ground black pepper
Fresh basil leaves

---

1. Thickly slice the aubergine and spread out on a plate. Sprinkle liberally with salt and leave to stand for 20 minutes.

2. Meanwhile, prepare the pizza dough according to the recipe and roll out to form a circle about 25cm/10-inches in diameter.

3. Place the dough on a lightly oiled baking sheet and prick all over with a fork.

4. Spread the base with the passata. Allow to stand in a warm place while preparing the topping.

5. Meanwhile, rinse the aubergine and pat dry. Heat about 4 tbsps olive oil in a large frying pan and fry the aubergine slices on both sides until beginning to brown. You may need to do this in batches; add extra olive oil as required.

6. Arrange alternate slices of aubergine and tomato on top of the pizza.

7. Sprinkle with garlic and season well. Tear the basil into pieces and scatter on top.

8. Drizzle with olive oil and bake in a preheated oven at 200°C/400°F/Gas Mark 6 for 25-30 minutes or until the base is cooked and golden.

TIME: Preparation takes about 20 minutes. Cooking takes approximately 40 minutes.

VARIATION: Top with any cheese of your choice

LEEK AND POTATO PIZZA

A tempting pizza which is a meal in itself.

MAKES ONE 23CM/9-INCH PIZZA

Full quantity Scone Based Dough
Full quantity Tomato Sauce
60g/2oz butter
225g/8oz potatoes, cubed
2 small leeks, sliced
Salt and freshly ground black pepper
120g/4oz Cheshire cheese, crumbled

1. Prepare the pizza dough according to the recipe and roll out to form a circle about 23cm/9-inches in diameter.

2. Place the dough on a lightly oiled baking sheet and prick all over with a fork.

3. Spread the base with the tomato sauce.

4. Melt the butter in a saucepan and sauté the cubed potatoes for about 5 minutes until beginning to brown. Remove from the pan and set aside.

5. Add the leeks and sauté for 2-3 minutes until just softened.

6. Return the potatoes to the pan and toss until well combined.

7. Spoon the leek and potato mixture over the pizza and season with salt and pepper.

8. Scatter the cheese over the pizza.

9. Bake in a preheated oven at 190°C/375°F/ Gas Mark 5 for 35-40 minutes or until the base is cooked and golden.

TIME: Preparation takes about 15 minutes. Cooking takes approximately 50 minutes.

PIZZA WITH FOUR CHEESES

A pizza for cheese fans, this recipe uses four Italian cheeses,
but you could use whichever cheese you like.

MAKES ONE 25CM/10-INCH PIZZA

Full quantity Basic Yeast Dough
Full quantity Tomato Sauce, preferably fresh
3 plum tomatoes, sliced
60g/2oz Gorgonzola cheese, cut into small
    chunks
60g/2oz Mozzarella cheese, sliced
60g/2oz Fontina or Bel paese cheese, sliced
    or cut into small chunks
60g/2oz Dolcelatte cheese, crumbled
Few fresh marjoram leaves, to garnish

1. Prepare the pizza dough according to the recipe and roll out to form a circle about 27.5cm/11-inches in diameter.

2. Place the dough on a lightly oiled baking sheet. Fold over the edges to form a raised border.

3. Spread with the tomato sauce and allow to stand in a warm place for 10-15 minutes.

4. Arrange the sliced tomato on top of the base and bake in a preheated oven at 200°C/400°F/Gas Mark 6 for 10 minutes.

5. Mark the pizza into four. Place the Gorgonzola on one section of the pizza.

6. Place the sliced Mozzarella on another section of the pizza.

7. Slice the Fontina or Bel Paese and place on the third section of the pizza

8. Sprinkle the Dolcelatte over the forth section.

9. Bake in a preheated oven at 200°C/400°F/ Gas Mark 6 for 15-20 minutes or until the base is cooked and golden and the cheese has melted.

10. Serve sprinkled with a few fresh marjoram leaves.

TIME: Preparation takes about 15 minutes. Cooking takes approximately 30 minutes.

SAVOURY VEGETABLE PIZZA

*Different from the usual vegetarian pizza, you can use up leftover vegetables
or start from fresh for this first rate dish.*

MAKES ONE 23CM/9-INCH PIZZA

Full quantity Scone Based Dough
Full quantity Tomato Sauce
120g/4oz cauliflower and broccoli florets
1 carrot, sliced
60g/2oz green beans, cut into short lengths
45g/1½oz butter
90g/3oz brown cap mushrooms, sliced
15g/½oz plain flour
140ml/¼pt milk
Salt and freshly ground black pepper
Pinch of freshly grated nutmeg
120g/4oz Double Gloucester cheese with
    chives and onion, grated

1. Prepare the pizza dough according to the recipe and roll out to form a circle a little larger than 25cm/10-inch in diameter.

2. Place the dough on a lightly oiled baking sheet. Fold over the edges to form a raised border.

3. Spread the tomato sauce over the pizza base. Allow to stand in a warm place for 15 minutes.

4. Bring a pan of lightly salted water to the boil and cook the cauliflower, broccoli, carrot and beans for 5 minutes. Refresh under cold water and drain well. Pile on top of the tomato sauce.

5. Melt the butter in a small saucepan and sauté the mushrooms for 2 minutes.

6. Stir in the flour and cook over a low heat for 1 minute.

7. Remove from the heat and gradually add the milk, stirring well after each addition.

8. Return to the heat and cook over a low heat until thickened, stirring constantly.

9. Season well with salt, pepper and nutmeg and stir in the cheese.

10. Spoon the sauce over the vegetables and bake in a preheated oven at 190°C/ 375°F/Gas Mark 5 for 35-40 minutes or until the base is cooked and golden.

TIME: Preparation takes about 15 minutes. Cooking takes approximately 50 minutes.

PIZZETTE
(MINI PIZZAS)

Mini pizzas are great for children and ideal at parties.

MAKES 8 MINI PIZZAS

Full quantity Basic Yeast Dough
Full quantity Tomato Sauce
Small bunch of spring onions, sliced
1 tbsp olive oil
60g/2oz mushrooms, sliced
2 gherkins, sliced
4 slices salami, cut into strips
60g/2oz red Leicester cheese, grated
60g/2oz Mozzarella cheese, grated
Chopped fresh oregano
Salt and freshly ground black pepper

1. Prepare the pizza dough according to the recipe.

2. Divide into eight and roll into smooth balls.

3. Roll out each ball to form a circle about 10cm/4 inches in diameter.

4. Place on a lightly oiled baking sheet and prick all over with a fork.

5. Spread the tomato sauce over each pizza base and allow to stand in a warm place while preparing the rest of the topping.

6. Scatter a few slices of spring onion onto each pizza.

7. Heat the oil in a small saucepan and sauté the mushrooms for 2 minutes until just softened. Arrange over four of the pizza bases.

8. Arrange the gherkins and salami on the remaining pizza bases.

9. Mix together the cheeses, oregano and seasoning and divide between the eight pizzas.

10. Bake in a preheated oven at 200°C/ 400°F/Gas Mark 6 for 20-25 minutes or until the bases are cooked and golden.

TIME: Preparation takes about 20 minutes. Cooking takes approximately 25 minutes.

VARIATION: For an instant mini pizza base, use toasted muffins, soft baps or crumpets. Bake them just long enough to melt the cheese, or cook under a preheated grill.

PIZZA FUNNY FACES

Encourage your children into the kitchen by letting them use their imagination to make their own pizza faces.

MAKES 4 MINI PIZZAS

Full quantity Scone Base Dough
90ml/6 tbsps passata
Selection of: sliced processed cheese, sliced
    Mozzarella cheese, grated Red Leicester
    cheese, cherry tomatoes, strips red or
    green pepper, button mushrooms, grated
    carrot, olives, mini gherkins

1. Prepare the pizza dough according to the recipe.

2. Divide into four and roll into smooth balls.

3. Roll out each ball to form a circle about 10cm/4-inches in diameter.

4. Place on a lightly oiled baking sheet and prick all over with a fork.

5. Bake in a preheated oven at 200°C/400°F/ Gas Mark 6 for 10 minutes, then reduce the heat to 180°C/350°F/Gas Mark 4. If your children are helping you, allow the bases to cool before proceeding.

6. Spread the passata over the part-baked pizza bases.

7. Make the faces from a selection of the ingredients. Let your imagination run riot or see photograph for ideas. Sliced cheese can be cut out to form features. Grated cheese or carrot are good for hair. Cherry tomatoes and olives (either black or stuffed green olives)are good for eyes. Gherkins and mushrooms are ideal for noses. Strips of pepper make great mouths.

8. Bake in the oven for 10-15 minutes or until the cheese melts.

TIME: Preparation takes about 30 minutes. Cooking takes approximately 30 minutes.

WATCHPOINT: Allow plenty of time for preparation if you have young helpers. Remember to supervise the use of sharp knives and the cooking itself.

PIZZA PRONTO

Need a pizza in a hurry? This prepared pizza base is much better than one which is frozen.

MAKES ONE 25CM/10-INCH PIZZA

1 x 25cm/10-inch ready-made pizza base
½ x 250g/8½oz jar pizza sauce
120g/4oz jar marinated peppers, drained
    weight or
120g/4oz can sliced mushrooms, drained
    weight
30g/1oz snack salami, cut into chunks,
    (optional)
120g/4oz pizza cheese (ready grated
    Mozzarella, smoked Mozzarella and
    Cheddar cheese, seasoned with herbs)

1. Place the pizza on a lightly oiled baking sheet and spread with the pizza sauce.

2. Arrange the vegetables, and salami if using, over the sauce and sprinkle with the grated cheese.

3. Bake in a preheated oven at 220°C/425°F/ Gas Mark 7 for 10-15 minutes or as directed on the pizza base packet.

TIME: Preparation takes about 5 minutes. Cooking takes approximately 15 minutes.

COOK'S TIP: If you cannot find pizza cheese, use grated Mozzarella or Cheddar cheese or a mixture of the two.

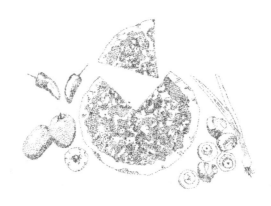

FRENCH BREAD PIZZA

French bread pizzas makes a delicious snack and a refreshing change from cheese on toast, they are also ideal for parties. Choose any combination of toppings.

SERVES 4

1 small French stick
90ml/6 tbsps tomato pizza or pasta sauce
Selection of: ham, pepperoni, salami, diced
    bacon, sliced mushrooms, sweetcorn,
    diced peppers, pineapple, chopped
    tomatoes or prawns
60g/2oz Mozzarella cheese, grated
60g/2oz Cheddar cheese, grated
Chopped fresh oregano

1. Cut the French stick in half lengthways and in half again to form four bases.

2. Cook the cut sides under a preheated grill until just toasted.

3. Spread the bases with pizza or pasta sauce and top with a selection of your choice.

4. Mix together the two cheeses and the oregano, and sprinkle over the pizza.

5. Place under the grill until the cheese melts and the toppings are heated through. Serve at once.

TIME: Preparation takes about 15 minutes. Cooking takes approximately 5 minutes.

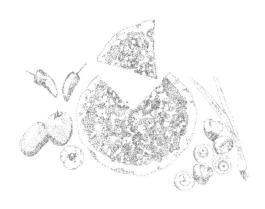

SUMMER FRUIT PIZZA

Pizza bases can be topped with sweet toppings too. This one is a delicious alternative to a fruit flan.

MAKES ONE 23CM/9-INCH PIZZA

Full quantity Scone Based Dough
120g/4oz raspberries
90g/3oz blackcurrants
90g/3oz redcurrants
2 tbsps caster sugar
2 tbsps water
1 tsp arrowroot
90ml/6 tbsps Mascarpone cheese

1. Prepare the pizza dough according to the recipe and roll out to form a circle a little larger than 23cm/9-inches in diameter.

2. Place the dough on a lightly oiled baking sheet and fold over the edges to form a raised border.

3. Bake in a preheated oven at 190°C/375°F/ Gas Mark 5 for 15 minutes until just golden.

4. Meanwhile, place the fruit in a saucepan with the sugar and 1 tbsp water. Cook gently for 2-3 minutes, stirring until the fruit just begins to soften and the juices run.

5. Mix the arrowroot with another 1 tbsp water and add to the pan. Continue to cook until the fruit thickens, stirring constantly.

6. Place blobs of Mascarpone cheese on the part-cooked pizza base.

7. Spoon over the fruit mixture.

8. Bake for 10-15 minutes or until the base is cooked and golden.

TIME: Preparation takes about 10 minutes. Cooking takes approximately 35 minutes.

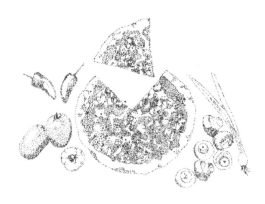

APPLE AND CINNAMON PIZZA

Wonderful served hot or cold.

MAKES ONE 23CM/9-INCH PIZZA

225g/8oz self-raising flour
90g/3oz margarine
90g/3oz caster sugar
30g/1oz ground almonds
1 egg yolk
45-60ml/3-4 tbsps milk
340g/12oz ricotta cheese
60g/2oz sultanas
Lemon juice
2-3 dessert apples, cored, sliced and tossed
    in lemon juice
1 tsp ground cinnamon
2 tbsps brandy (optional)

1. Sift the flour into a mixing bowl. Rub in the margarine until the mixture resembles fine breadcrumbs.

2. Stir in 30g/1oz of the sugar and the almonds.

3. Add the egg yolk and enough milk to form a soft dough.

4. Shape into a smooth round ball and roll out to form a circle a little larger than 23cm/9-inches in diameter.

5. Place the dough on a lightly oiled baking sheet and fold over the edges to form a raised border.

6. Beat together the cheese, sultanas, remaining sugar and 1tbsp lemon juice until well combined.

7. Spread over the pizza base.

8. Arrange the apple slices on the pizza. Sprinkle with cinnamon and the brandy, if using.

9. Bake in a preheated oven at 190°C/375°F/ Gas Mark 5 for 35-40 minutes or until the base is cooked and golden.

TIME: Preparation takes about 30 minutes. Cooking takes approximately 40 minutes.

STRAWBERRY AND ALMOND PIZZA

*You can use the scone base for this pizza but a biscuit base
makes it a lovely summer dessert.*

MAKES ONE 20CM/8-INCH PIZZA

90g/3oz self-raising flour
45g/1½oz ground almonds
45g/1½oz caster sugar
60g/2oz butter
2 tbsps strawberry jam
225g/8oz ricotta cheese
30g/1oz light muscovado sugar
1 tbsp Amaretti liqueur
225g/8oz strawberries
Sprigs fresh mint, to decorate

1. Sift the flour into a mixing bowl. Stir in the almonds.

2. Stir in the sugar, then rub the butter into the mixture. Work the mixture together with your hands until it forms a soft dough.

3. Place in a lightly greased 20cm/8-inch round, loose-bottomed cake tin and press out to cover completely the base of the tin. Prick the dough with a fork.

4. Bake in a preheated oven at 180°C/350°F/ Gas Mark 4 for 10-12 minutes until golden.

5. Allow to cool, then transfer to a serving dish.

6. Spread the pizza base with the strawberry jam.

7. Beat together the cheese, muscovado sugar and liqueur, and spread over the pizza base.

8. Arrange the strawberries on top of the pizza. Decorate with fresh mint.

TIME: Preparation takes about 15 minutes. Cooking takes approximately 12 minutes.

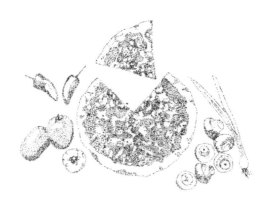

BANANA PIZZA

A super sweet pizza that is best eaten hot and fresh. It does not reheat well.

MAKES ONE 25CM/10-INCH PIZZA

Full quantity of Basic Yeast Dough
6 large bananas, sliced and tossed in lemon
    juice
90g/3oz light muscovado sugar

---

1. Prepare the pizza dough according to the recipe and roll out to form a circle a little larger than 25cm/10-inches in diameter.

2. Place the dough on a lightly oiled baking sheet. Fold over the edges to form a raised border. Allow to stand in a warm place for 15 minutes.

3. Arrange the sliced banana on top of the pizza.

4. Sprinkle with the sugar and bake in a preheated oven at 200°C/400°F/Gas MArk 6 for 25-30 minutes or until the base is cooked and golden. Allow to cool slightly before serving.

TIME: Preparation takes about 15 minutes. Cooking takes approximately 30 minutes.

CHOC 'N MARSHMALLOW

Popular with children, this sweet pizza is a treat to savour.

MAKES ONE 23CM/9-INCH PIZZA

225g/8oz plain flour
90g/3oz margarine
1 egg yolk
About 60ml/4 tbsps milk
120g/4oz plain chocolate, broken into
    squares
60g/2oz butter
1 tbsp cocoa powder
2 tbsp icing sugar
120g/4oz marshmallows

---

1. Sift the flour into a mixing bowl. Rub in the margarine until the mixture resembles fine breadcrumbs.

2. Add the egg yolk and enough milk to form a soft dough.

3. Shape into a smooth round ball and roll out to form a circle a little larger than 23cm/9-inches in diameter.

4. Place on a lightly oiled baking sheet and fold over the edges to form a raised border.

5. Bake in a preheated oven at 200°C/400°F/ Gas Mark 6 for 15 minutes or until just golden. Reduce the heat to 180°C/350°F/ Gas Mark 4.

6. Meanwhile, place the chocolate in a small bowl along with the butter. Heat gently over a bowl of simmering water, stirring until the chocolate and butter have melted and are well combined.

7. Beat the cocoa powder and icing sugar into the mixture.

8. Spread the chocolate sauce over the part-cooked pizza base and arrange the marshmallows on top.

9. Return to the oven for 10 minutes or until the marshmallows begin to melt. Allow to cool slightly before serving.

TIME: Preparation takes about 15 minutes. Cooking takes approximately 25 minutes.

Index